It's Cool To BE an OMie

Debbie Bard

AuthorHouse™
1663 Liberty Drive
Bloomington, IN 47403
www.authorhouse.com
Phone: 1 (800) 839-8640

Published by AuthorHouse 05/09/2019

ISBN: 978-1-7283-0275-1 (sc)
ISBN: 978-1-7283-0277-5 (hc)
ISBN: 978-1-7283-0276-8 (e)

Library of Congress Control Number: 2019902641

Print information available on the last page.

authorHOUSE®

It's Cool to BE an OMie

For my husband, Dave, and MY 4 little OMies, Jett, Jade, Jewel and Jem. You are ALL my support staff and the true definition of what it means to be an OMie. I truly adore you and your love awakens my soul.

For all the present and future OMies…. Spread the Love!

An OMie's smile is their best accessory. It's the first thing they put on every morning.

They know the most important person
to take care of is their self.
They also know that they can care for
their self by caring for others.

An OMie ALWAYS spreads kindness and is
ALWAYS sending out good vibes to ALL.

They do ALL things with love. They know that there
is no such thing as too much awesOMeness.

An OMie knows that gratitude is the best attitude.

They know that there is ALWAYS
something to be thankful for!!!

An OMie is ALWAYS eager to learn.

They know that not all classrooms have four
walls and that the world is theirs to explore.

An OMie is ALWAYS honest.

They know that if they are honest, they never have to remember what they say.

An OMie knows that fear is NOT a factor.

They are ALWAYS up for adventure and
ALWAYS excited to try new things.

An OMie loves their cOMmunity
and is giving of their time.

They know it's super cool to volunteer.
They are aware of the ripple effect that
they can create with their actions.

An OMie dreams BIG...real BIG!

They know that ANYthing and EVERYthing is possible.

An OMie ALWAYS uses their voice for good.

They know words are powerful and that they
are the keeper of their own behavior.

An OMie understands that the
mind is a powerful tool.

They know the importance of chillin' like an
OMie. They believe that within them, they
have the power to rise above ANY situation
to become the brightest version of their self.

An OMie ALWAYs loves and cares for Mother Earth.

They are proud to be an eco-warrior.
They recycle, reduce, and reuse.

An OMie picks flowers NOT fights.

They stop to smell them too!

An OMie knows that good energy
rocks and that it is contagious.

They effortlessly spread peace, love, and happiness.

An OMie loves to give hugs….
especially to the trees!

They know the importance of trees to the
planet. The forest is their playground.

An OMie ALWAYS treats their body with respect.

They eat healthy, drink lots of water, and YOgatate.

An OMie is ALWAYS a great friend.

They operate on SOULer energy and use their
positive energy to connect with others.

It's cool to BE an OMie.

The world needs more OMies...
peace, love, happiness, earth.

Calling All OMies

My Little OMies started as a mission to empower OUR YOUth to love themselves, their cOMmunity, and Mother Nature. My Little OMies embraces the practice of yoga and the power of nature to better the mind, body, and soul. Our goal is to raise responsible, honest, and compassionate little yogis. Our hope is to lead the OMies to a world centric view of humanity and to do ALL things with LOVE! Join Team OMie and BE a part of an enlightened generation.
For more info visit www.mylittleomies.com
or
Follow us on Facebook, Twitter, Instagram, and Pinterest

"If every eight-year-old in the world is taught meditation, we will eliminate violence from within the world in one generation". Dalai Lama

"If WE are to teach real peace in the world, and WE are to carry on a real war against war, we shall have to begin with the children." Ghandi

About the Author

The creator of *My Little OMies*, Debbie, has a passion for kids, yoga, and life. Debbie graduated Summa Cum Laude from Kent State University and holds a degree in middle childhood education. She is a certified children's yoga Instructor and life coach. Debbie has coached and continues to coach various sports at the high school, middle school, and youth levels. She is also involved with numerous charity and volunteer events. She loves to travel and dreams of having friends from all over the world who are doing BIG things to expand the consciousness of the human race. Debbie believes in the power of energy and vows to use hers to have a profound impact on the betterment of humanity. She is happily married and raising 4 little OMie's of her own.

Printed in the United States
By Bookmasters